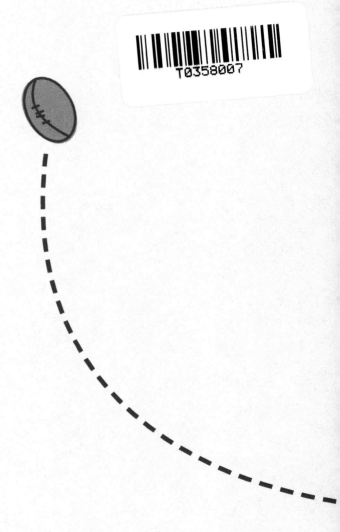

KICKING GOALS

with Goodesy and Magic

Anita Heiss

with

Adam Goodes

&

Michael O'Loughlin

Piccolo
NERO

Published by Nero,
an imprint of Schwartz Books Pty Ltd
Wurundjeri Country
22–24 Northumberland Street
Collingwood VIC 3066, Australia
enquiries@blackincbooks.com
www.nerobooks.com

9781863958530 (paperback)
9781925435139 (ebook)

A catalogue record for this
book is available from the
National Library of Australia

Cover design by Peter Long
Photographs on cover and pages 87 and 89 by Paul Leonardo
Photograph on page 85 by Amanda James
Text design and typesetting by Tristan Main
Cartoons by Phillip Marsden

Printed in Australia by McPherson's Printing Group.

contents

contents

Introduction 6

CHAPTER ONE
Who's the funniest one (is) isn't it? 9

CHAPTER TWO
Growing up popular 23

CHAPTER THREE
Getting called to the principal's office 41

CHAPTER FOUR
I didn't want to be a bully player:
to stop it when it does?

CHAPTER FIVE
Having spirit 83

CHAPTER SIX
Learning the way 97

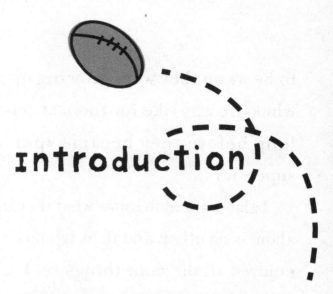

Introduction

Adam Goodes and Michael O'Loughlin are AFL legends, admired and respected around Australia not only because they can kick a football, but also because they are just really great fellas. What some people mightn't know is that they are also good mates. Oh, and they are family, too!

I thought it would be fun to sit down with them and find out what they wanted to be when they were growing up and what life was like for them at school, long before they became sporting superstars.

I also wanted to know what they liked about each other, and if, as friends, they enjoyed all the same things. So I asked them exactly the same questions, but separately. Michael didn't know what Adam said, and vice versa.

It was fun, and I learned a lot about how important their friends were in helping them to reach their goals. You probably have a special friend, or maybe a cousin, who you hang out with, and maybe call when you have exciting news, or when you feel sad or angry. That's when we need our friends the most, don't you think?

Of course, Adam and Michael both played for the Sydney Swans. Michael wore the number 19 and Adam wore the number 37. They were both recognised for their contributions to the game in different ways. Adam won the Brownlow Medal – not once, but twice (in 2003 and 2006)! It's the most fancy-pants award you can get in the AFL. And Michael was inducted into the AFL Hall of Fame in 2015 – that's the highest honour you can receive once you've retired.

In 2014 Adam was named Australian of the Year, and today he and Michael run their own foundation called the

GO Foundation, which provides scholarships to help Indigenous kids go to school.

CHAPTER ONE

who's the funniest and the fastest?

Michael and Adam are family, but they are also great mates. What do they think is the difference between family and friends, and what else do you need besides a good mate?

ADAM: If I was stranded on a desert island with Michael I would definitely take my headphones. Everyone needs some time on their own, and if Michael kept talking to me I could just put them on and zone out. Michael likes to talk A LOT! The other thing I'd take would be a satellite phone, so I could call someone to get me off the island.

MICHAEL: If I were stranded on a desert island with Adam, I'd take a football and a spear gun to catch fish. That's our mob's way.

ADAM: Michael and I call each other cuz or bruz, and we have some other nicknames too. I call him Magic and he calls me Goodsey or the Godfather, because I am godfather to his children.

My other nickname is 'X Factor'. One day, after I kicked a few goals and I was walking off the ground, the boys heard me muttering to myself and thought that I was saying 'the difference'. From then on they called me 'The Difference' or 'The X Factor', because they said that I was the difference between us winning or losing. As a kid I was called Roy, because that's my middle name.

MICHAEL: As a kid, on the field I was always just called Mick. When I got to Sydney they gave me the nickname Magic, which then became Majo. One guy at training said I had something like magic and it just stuck.

It's an awesome nickname! Sometimes they aren't so great — there's one guy on the team called Booger! Everyone now calls me Micky O or Majo. Even my kids will say, 'Micky O, I'm hungry.'

I call Adam 'The Godfather' because he's the godfather of my kids. He knows that if something happens to me they're his responsibility — like it or not, he's got to look after them. And my kids are obsessed with him — we catch up at least once a week.

ADAM: When you're at school, your friends are people you share things in common with, or perhaps you're just in the same class. Some people might be your friend because they live next door to you, or they might even like the sports you play. Other friends can be people you're in a team with. So there are lots of different ways you can become friends.

When you're older, friendship is often about sharing common interests, but it's also about your morals — what you like and dislike. You become more aware of what people say and how they treat people. Basically, I want to be around people who treat others well. I want to be around people who care for others the same way I do.

MICHAEL: Friendships change over time. When you grow up your goals change, and you decide who you want to be. You think about whether you want to be like your parents or your cousins, and so you change how you behave.

I knew that if I wanted to play sport I couldn't go and smoke. I couldn't go out drinking with my mates all night. I knew I had to train. I didn't really realise that by choosing those things, it meant I wasn't making bad decisions like stealing cars. Some kids chose to steal cars; I knew that if I did that I wouldn't be playing football. I wasn't an angel but I knew the difference between right and wrong. I had to go to school to play football.

It helped that my friends growing up liked football, because I wouldn't have been able to go to half the games if their parents hadn't driven me. But that's also where I was very single-minded, because it didn't matter if my friends played footy or not, I would still go and train and play because I loved what I was doing.

ADAM: You can still be friends with people who don't like the same things as you. Take Michael, for instance: we are great mates, but I like playing cards and golf, and he doesn't. That's probably because he's not very good at them!

MICHAEL: Adam likes golf; I don't like golf. He likes cards and can play for hours by himself. I'd rather watch a movie or read a good book. It doesn't mean our friendship is any lesser for it.

One of Adam's really great strengths is that he invests time in his relationships with people. He's probably the best at it that I've ever seen. That's how friendships are sustained.

ADAM: I still have friends who say things that I don't agree with, but I always tell them if they want to continue being my friend, they have to make better choices about what they say and when they say it.

For me, it's about being honest. If your good friend says or does something you don't agree with, or makes you feel sad or angry, then you should talk about it with them.

MICHAEL: Now, as a grown-up, friendship is different. It's about raising a family and leading a happy life. But to achieve that, you've got to work hard, stay in school and eat the right foods. I think most people just want to be happy, do the right thing and find a girl to marry — or a boy!

Adam's friendship means a lot to me. The toughest moment for me was the death of my grandmother, and Adam was really solid. With those types of things, and with my family living thousands of miles away, you need to be able to rely on each other.

What Adam went through when people booed at games was really bad. I didn't know what to do but I knew I had to be there. We constantly told each other we loved each other.

ADAM: My first memory of Michael was watching him play for the Sydney Swans on television on a Sunday afternoon. I was about fifteen or sixteen years old, sitting in my living room in Horsham. I thought he was a good player and he kicked a lot of exciting goals. It was good seeing him running around and being one of only a couple of blackfellas on TV. It was really amazing to see such a young player doing so well.

The first time Michael and I spoke was when he called me the day after I was drafted to the Swans. He called to say congratulations and that he was looking forward to meeting up in Sydney. Then he said, 'By the way, did you know that we are cousins?'

I asked my mum if we were related and she said, 'Yes, he's your cousin.' It was so much nicer going to Sydney knowing there would be a family member waiting for me, to show me the ropes.

I don't have a big brother, and our dad was in and out of our lives from an early age, plus I had my stepdad for a few years before he and my mother separated. So to know that I'd have a male in Sydney to help look after me, who'd have my back, that was good to know.

MICHAEL: My first memory of Adam is hearing his name being read out at the Sydney Swans footy club. I'd been at the Swans for four years.

It was 1997. I was at home in Adelaide. After every season you get eight weeks off, so you pack your bags and go home. I'd go home and catch up with friends and we'd hang out and party.

You always watch the draft because you want to know who's coming in. Adam's name got read out, and then Mum told me he was my relation. He's my Aunty Lisa's son.

Then up flashed a picture of Goodesy and I saw that he was a blackfella with a beard and long hair. I thought he looked like he was twenty-two, but he was only seventeen.

Mum dug up his phone number, and because we had no phone I went down to the phone box and put my forty cents in and said, 'Is this Adam?'

'Yeah, who's this?'

'It's Michael O'Loughlin.'

'No way!'

'Yeah, we're related.'

'I know, Mum's been telling me all about it. '

'I can't wait to see you in Sydney in a few weeks.'

And that was it. I remember being in that phone box to this day. Adam and I have been tight since he arrived in Sydney.

Technically speaking, though, Adam is actually my uncle! His grandmother and my great-grandmother were sisters.

ADAM: The difference between family and friends is that you that can't get away from family— you see them all the time at events like barbecues, weddings and funerals. But a friend is something else; you can choose when you see that person. I think friendship is a lot more about choices— who you choose to be your friend, and what you like and don't like about them when you see them.

With family, whatever happens, for good or bad, you're all in with that person, you never cut them off and you have to do what you can to help them. Blood is thicker than water.

And Michael and I are very close. We've played football together for eleven years.

MICHAEL: The only real difference between a cousin and your mate is maybe that a cuz is a bit closer because he's your blood. When you're a kid and your mum says, 'Look after your cousins while I go to the shop,' you just do it because you know they're your family and you're in trouble if you don't. And I knew that early because I grew up with the mob.

When my cousins come to Sydney, I go and meet them for dinner or coffee and I tell them where to go in Sydney. I try to make them feel included.

ADAM: Friendship and family are about support. They're about the people who are going to be by your side. For me, Michael has been there all through the journey; whether it's helping me on the field, or family stuff off the field, Michael has been there. His support and encouragement helped me become the person I am. He always has my back: he is my family.

I respect Michael and his opinion. I have never had an older brother, and Michael was that person for me.

Sharing life's experiences with each other has strengthened that bond. I've been there for the birth of all but one of Michael's children.

MICHAEL: What I learned at the Sydney Swans is that the team is only as good as the younger players coming through. You're only as strong as your weakest link. The AFL is completely the opposite of a corporate work environment, where a young guy comes in, but he doesn't get mentored in a way that will see him take the CEO's job. It doesn't happen in business. In the AFL, it was my job to mentor someone to take my place.

I was only twenty when Adam came to Sydney, and he was seventeen. I was going into my third year when he was going into his first year. We played eleven years together.

Over the years, we've spent time together on and off the field. Everything from going to the movies, going out for dinner. In the early days we spent time together learning how to be elite players, because we were both young when we arrived at the Swans and neither of us knew how to be a professional, or how to train like a professional. So that was something we learned to do together.

Being at the Swans was like being part of a massive family — especially in

Sydney, because we were all away from our homes. The majority of people were from different states; when I was there we only had three people from Sydney.

ADAM: Michael loves to joke around. He loves to give it out, but if you come back at him with some banter he is doubly quick at coming back at you. Michael is the funniest out of the two of us. He likes to joke a lot and he tells a good yarn. But he doesn't like people making fun of him at all, which makes him really quick. He's always good at responding with a witty comeback.

MICHAEL: I am easily the funniest because my wit is quicker!

ADAM: I'm definitely the fastest on the field. Unfortunately, Michael aged quickly because of his knees, but he did extremely well with his body the last couple of years when his knees were good.

MICHAEL: Goodesy is the fastest! I've got old knees. Adam's greatest strength is his athleticism.

ADAM: We've both got nice tanned skin, so we both look exceptionally good in the red-and-white, but I'd have to say I probably look better with my tight shorts. Michael wore really baggy shorts, and they didn't look great. I know he also wears baggy speedos underneath – and trust me, that's not a good look either!

MICHAEL: I'd have to say I look the best in the red and white. I was runner-up in a Bachelor of the Year award.

ADAM: If I was asked to describe Michael in three words, I would say he is caring, honest and disciplined.

MICHAEL: I'd say Adam is loyal, humble and classy.

ADAM: I'd have to say I am the best-looking, simply because I smile in photos. Michael doesn't really like to smile.

MICHAEL: Please! I'm not as good-looking as a Wiggle, but I'm the best-looking out of Adam and me!

ADAM: Michael is the cheekiest for sure. He is forever playing games and teasing his kids, poking and prodding them. He is always up for a laugh.

MICHAEL: I'm not a massive prankster but if I see someone wearing silly shoes I'll say something. I might call them Ronald McDonald. The thing I miss most about playing footy is the locker room. It's where you get to know people more intimately. We do everything together: eat, sleep, shower. It's where we talk about what we did on the weekend.

ADAM: If Michael and I were ever going to compete for anything, I reckon it would be for the last piece of chocolate!

MICHAEL: There's nothing I'd compete with Adam for off the field. Maybe we'd compete to get in front of the mirror.

ADAM: The funniest moment we've had together was when I caught my first fish. We were fishing in Brazil and it was really hard putting mincemeat on a hook! It was good bait, though, and a piranha just jumped up and took it right away! We cooked the fish and ate them, and even though they were bony, the meat was tasty. We had a great time.

MICHAEL: Well, it's not funny, but Adam helped me meet my wife, Emma. I fell in love with her the night I met her, and he got her number for me. I called her the next day and that was that.

CHAPTER TWO

Growing up sporty!

It didn't matter where Adam and Michael were going to grow up, they were always going to play sport.

ADAM: I grew up in a lot of different places. My family moved around a fair bit when I was a kid, moving closer and then further away from the extended family. Being the oldest was tough growing up. I was supposed to know better, and I was always punished for the mistakes my brothers made. It was nice to be the man of the house but it came with high expectations.

I spent a lot of my childhood in Horsham, in Victoria, and I remember always being in the backyard playing cricket, volleyball and tennis with my two younger brothers, Jake and Brett. It was great fun having younger brothers: we spent so much of our time outside, playing games, riding our bikes, swimming in the river. The camaraderie we had with each other was great. Of course, we didn't have computer games back them. Sometimes we just had a tennis ball and a bit of stick, and maybe a cricket bat if we were lucky, but we were always able to entertain ourselves for hours on end.

After school and on the weekends, it was all about sports. If it got too hot, we might climb a tree or build a cubby house. If we were lucky we'd go to the river and grab onto the swing rope, swinging right over the river and dropping into the water. We had the river and we had dams, and we also had the local pool in Mildura. The best part of the pool was jumping off the towers, which were five and ten metres high.

MICHAEL: I grew up in Adelaide, in South Australia, in a suburb called Salisbury North, about twenty to thirty minutes north of the city. There was a big Aboriginal population there, the Kuarna mob. The majority of my mob are from Point Pearce, which is the home of the Narunga people, my mother's country. Then on my father's side are the Ngarrindjeri people, who come from the shores of Lake Alexandrina in the Coorong.

These are two big communities that have moved away from their own traditional lands to be closer to Adelaide, either for school or work or whatever it might be. Both communities were only a couple of hours away from our house, so it was easy to get in the car and go back and spend long weekends. It seemed like every holiday I was back on community, riding motorbikes, fishing, chasing rabbits. They would pile us on a community truck that had been used to move dirt that day, and then at night we'd put a spotlight out and there'd be fifty kids in the back of the truck. I did that from about eight to thirteen years of age — we were mostly boys, but there were girls there too.

We had a shack outside our community as well, and we'd stay there and there would be people everywhere. It was awesome! You were never alone.

Living in Salisbury North, I went to school every day, but the biggest thing in that community was that everyone played sport. People played netball or AFL, and some chucked a basketball around. When the footy wasn't on after school we were out on the street kicking a ball.

My mum was involved in education, so she was always saying, 'Do your homework!' Sometimes I may have told a little lie and said that I'd finished it, because I knew that if my homework was done then I could go outside and kick the football around until the sun went down. My brother and I would kick it on the road we lived on, but if a bus or car came along we would get off.

Our mates and cousins lived around the corner, and we would go and play basketball and shoot hoops at school. It seemed like every day we were playing cricket in the backyard or something else. We were always playing sport.

CHAPTER THREE

Getting called to the principal's office

Adam and Michael weren't saints at school, but they didn't get into too much mischief and they reckon they both learned their lessons, or at least knew when they did something wrong. What do you think? Are they telling the truth?

ADAM: I was called to the principal's office. I think he wanted me to tell on whoever put a hole in the wall. I knew who did it, but I didn't want my friend to get in trouble. I'd been friends with these guys for a couple of years since I moved high schools.

I knew that we were probably all in the wrong because we'd been wrestling each other in the hallway. We were just being a little bit—okay, we were being *very* — silly. Then one boy got thrown into the wall, and that's how the hole happened.

We didn't agree to stay quiet, but you just knew that the other guys wouldn't say it was you, and you wouldn't say it was them. For me it was about being loyal, but also about being honest.

I don't think I was being dishonest to the principal by not telling him who was there. I really didn't want to get my friends in trouble. But at the same time, I wanted the friend who caused the hole to put his hand up and take responsibility. I thought by being quiet I was giving him the opportunity to stand up, because I'd learned that when you do something wrong it's good to take responsibility for your actions.

I didn't really get into *that* much mischief at school, but I did make some mistakes. I remember once I went on a field trip to the zoo and the teacher specifically told us *not* to make eye contact with the gorilla. But... well, me and a friend thought it would be a good idea to do the exact opposite of what we were told, so we climbed up on the ledge, looked into the enclosure and made eye contact with the gorilla.

When you stare at a gorilla, it actually means you are challenging them. Of course, I didn't know that at the time – I was just doing it because they told us not to – but I later learned that's the way gorillas communicate with each other.

And so, on that day, the gorilla started beating his chest, running around and throwing bamboo at us. We just laughed because we got a reaction. We thought it was funny. But then the teacher saw what we were doing and we got in trouble. It wasn't until I learned more about gorillas that I realised it was actually very bad behaviour on our part.

MICHAEL: We smashed so many windows as kids playing ball sports, whether it was cricket in the backyard or kicking the football around. I nearly got run over a few times kicking the ball on the road, but I got pretty good at ducking and dodging. I think the thing that upset our parents the most back then was when we'd get in the back of their nice cars covered in mud after a game.

We'd get in trouble after school from the security guards because we'd play chasey on the roof. They never caught us — we were too quick! We'd also hang out at the shops and eat chips.

The neighbourhood I grew up in was pretty tough, and very multicultural back in the day. There were a lot of Vietnamese and Aboriginal people, and Italians. We had to learn how to recognise who was trouble, and we kept out of trouble by being involved in sport.

ADAM: The truth is I always liked school because I enjoyed making friends. I enjoyed talking to people, getting to know people and watching people, but it was hard because we changed schools a fair bit. I reckon I went to five different primary schools and two high schools.

In primary school I had two teachers when I was in grades four and five. They shared the responsibility for us in those years, and they were our sports teachers as well. The best thing was whenever we finished our work quickly we were allowed to go outside and play sports and games, so it was a real big motivator for us to do our work, and do it well. It was the way the teachers rewarded us. I remember those being really fun times. I think a lot of kids, including myself, just wanted to be outside playing. I think most kids today still genuinely want to run around outside and burn energy.

MICHAEL: I liked school. I liked my mates and the friendships I made. The guys I played football with were the guys I went to school with, so we were all mates instantly. And sport was big for me because I was half-decent at it.

But it didn't really matter what sport it was, if you were half-decent at anything you'd be picked first or second and then people wanted to be around you. I found that transition really easy.

I was a bit of ratbag but never in serious trouble or anything, just like a normal kid. Get in trouble, sit in the corner for five minutes, go to detention. I was always talking in class. I made spitballs with paper and a straw.

I never really did anything really naughty at school, though. It was more things like throwing the football around in class — though one day someone dropped it and it smashed a window.

I knew what kind of trouble I'd be in when I got home if I did anything really bad. My mum was big on discipline; she ran the show and her word was the law. The biggest threat I got, the thing that frightened me most, was being told I couldn't play football on the weekend.

CHAPTER FOUR

I didn't want to be a footy player to start with ...

Sometimes when we are young, we dream about what we might be when we grow up. Quite often, what we want to be when we are ten years old is not the same thing we want when we get older, or what we end up being as an adult. What did Adam and Michael want to be as kids?

ADAM: When I was a kid, I wanted to be Michael Jordan, the basketball player. I had posters of him all over one wall. I liked how he did a slam-dunk, and I wanted to be just like him.

I played soccer until I was thirteen or fourteen years old, when we moved from Adelaide to a place called Burbank, in country Victoria. When we got there, there were no junior soccer teams, only a senior soccer team, and the game we were watching was very aggressive and there was a lot of bad language being used on the field. I was a young kid and my mum didn't want me to get involved in that.

It so happened that there was a game of AFL being played on another oval nearby, and I walked over and asked what it was about. It was the under-14s, and it was perfect. If I'd stuck with soccer, though, I reckon I could have been Australia's Lionel Messi!

MICHAEL: I always wanted to be an NBA basketballer! It's a fast game, and it's about coordination. I was inspired by Michael Jordan and other athletes in the US. I played basketball as a young child and fell in love with the game.

ADAM: The best thing about playing junior sport is that you get to give everything a try — different sports and different positions. If I was good in one sport, then why not try another sport? I liked challenging myself and learning something new — that was always how I felt about it.

MICHAEL: I was obsessed with football. Everywhere I went I had a ball. So if Mum said, 'Go get the milk,' I'd take a ball with me. I'd kick it against a pole or a tree, I'd bounce and run, I'd kick the ball up to myself. So without realising it, I was doing what most sporting organisations today say you need to do if you want to be an elite athlete: you have to have done a good 10,000 hours of sport. Now I teach the young kids at the football club that it's what you do away from training that matters.

So we would kick the ball at training, kick it on the way home, we'd kick the ball at night, we'd kick in the hallway — and whoever touched the wall was out. I didn't realise we were doing the right thing at that stage; we were just having fun kicking the ball.

I was a mad Carlton supporter. I was about twelve or thirteen and I was hooked. I watched footy religiously, every day, every weekend. Back in those days I watched the VFL, and then it became the AFL. I would watch and go, 'I'd like to do that,' but little did I know you could actually make a living out of it. It was just a dream of playing on TV. I didn't know how to get there; I didn't know what the journey would look like. It was just about getting in and playing. I didn't know you could get paid to do it.

What I loved most about watching footy on TV was that it was the highest level. I knew that if you were good, you could play in that league.

I remember holding the banner up for the local league in South Australia. It was for the Central District Bulldogs. My uncle played there, so he was a role model for me. The next step from the local league was playing in the AFL or VFL. I sort of knew there was a process, but you still had to be half-decent to get there.

I think for us little blackfellas growing up in Salisbury North, no one could afford golf clubs or a tennis racket. But a footy was five bucks, and so everyone played footy, and that's why the sport is such a success in the community. You can go anywhere and kick a ball. There were no tennis courts where I was from, and golf courses cost money, but you can go in the yard or on the oval and kick a ball. Or if there's a basketball hoop up, you can play that. That's the environment I grew up in — where we made use of what was available to us. For us it was a football.

ADAM: I was about eighteen when I decided I wanted to play AFL seriously. When I played AFL I played back, forward, ruck, rover and wingman. There aren't many positions I didn't play with the Sydney Swans, but I really loved playing in the midfield because I wanted to be near the action.

I liked being in a position where you had the most influence on the team winning or losing. I didn't like sitting on the bench much, but the good thing about today's game is you're only on the bench for a minute or two before you're back on the field. These days you're not on the bench for the wrong reason — it's more about rotating the players to get a rest.

I was sent off once. I elbowed somebody in the back when they weren't looking. It wasn't an accident — I deliberately struck him on the back. I was reported by the umpires and missed a game because of my actions. There was no excuse for what I did, and I got a one-week suspension. I deserved the week out and I learned my lesson.

MICHAEL: I didn't care where I played. The good players played up forward or in the middle. I played midfield and forward throughout my whole juniors.

The backline players get it pretty tough. They are always chasing someone else around. I like being chased.

CHAPTER FIVE
Kicking goals

ADAM: I remember kicking my first goal. It was my first ever game for the Sydney Swans, back in 1999. I was nineteen. It was round one, and we were playing against Port Adelaide at the Sydney Cricket Ground. It felt great.

It was a set shot, so I marked the ball and went back to do my run-up. I knew my mum and my two brothers were in the crowd watching. It was a really enjoyable moment and I remember thinking I was glad I could share it with them.

I remember kicking my last goal, too. It was against North Melbourne at ANZ Stadium in the 2015 Semi Final. I kicked two goals that day and I kicked the last goal of the game, but we lost by twenty-six points.

MICHAEL: I like kicking goals. I remember my first game. I was seven and playing in the under-9s for the local club with my cousin. I played the last few games of that year with the under-9s. I kicked three goals as a seven-year-old and I think everyone thought I was okay. My mum, my grandparents, and my uncles and aunts were all watching. It felt really good and I won a pair of socks! It was a big deal at that age.

When my cousin changed teams to the Salisbury North Hawks, I went too. It was walking distance from our house and I stayed there till I was drafted.

ADAM: It's not all about kicking goals. For me, I think the best thing about being in a team is that everybody in the team relies on you, and you rely on them. If someone makes a mistake, the next player has the opportunity to clean it up.

I also like that when you do something that is not up to your usual standard, you have other players there to support you and challenge you to make sure you do better the next time.

MICHAEL: The best thing about being in a team is that everyone relies on everyone else to get a good outcome — which is to win a game of football. You can't win a game of football by yourself! You have to involve the rest of the team. It doesn't matter what skill level they are at, if the team is going to succeed then they've all got to contribute.

It doesn't matter if you're the best player — you share the ball, you can't be a hog. I think I was a team player, but there would be times when the coaches would tell me to just kick the ball. You learn quickly as a kid what you can and can't do, and what other people can and can't do. You need to be unselfish.

ADAM: The most challenging thing about being a leader is trying to get the best out of others. When you are in a leadership role, you have to talk to other players, you have to challenge them on things they need to improve on. But at the end of the day, it's their choice. You can't force people to do something.

In the AFL we have something that's called 'one in, all in', which means if one person stuffs up, everyone gets punished. And that means we have to take extra care with what we do, because we are responsible for what happens to other people.

MICHAEL: In the AFL, if one person is late, everyone is punished. Everyone gets cranky, but everyone in the team also ends up being that person at one time or another. No one ever wants to be that person, though! In business, people just start without you if are ten minutes late. One of the biggest lessons I've learned in life is not to be late!

ADAM: Be present. When we are present we see everything we are supposed to.

MICHAEL: Every day I smile and laugh, even when things are bad. People might be doing it tough, but I refuse not to be positive.

CHAPTER SIX
Leading the way

Both Michael and Adam are leaders in the AFL and the wider community, but who do they look up to? And what do they think it takes to be a good leader?

ADAM: A good leader leads by example. They sacrifice their own personal agenda, their own ego, for what's best for the group. A leader is someone who also takes time to care for, support and challenge his team, and most importantly follow up after any incidents. I think a leader is also someone who, when the pressure is on, can perform their role no matter what is happening off the field.

MICHAEL: A good leader is someone who leads by example and uses their own specific leadership abilities; some guys are really good talkers, some are more 'follow me and I'll show you how to do it'.

ADAM: Everyone is a leader. I think a kid at school can be a leader by being the best student he or she can possibly be. When other people are mucking around and not doing what the teacher wants, they can ask their fellow students why they're doing it. They can ask: *Don't you want to learn? Don't you want to be good at something?*

Kids can also be leaders by helping others who might be struggling to learn. If you're really good at something, you can help teach other people your skills.

A leader also stands up for people who are being bullied. They help their friends by telling a teacher or another adult, not by watching and doing nothing. Doing nothing is not acceptable. I think helping and supporting a person who is being bullied takes real courage.

MICHAEL: When I was growing up, my mum and my uncle Wilbur Wilson were unbelievable role models. My uncle worked all his life — family came first. I also looked up to my grandparents, who made sure there was food on the table, clean shirts and shorts, and an immaculate house — which they ruled with an iron fist. I was very fortunate to have these people to look up to.

As I got older, I watched telly and saw Michael Jordan, and I started to think I wanted to be that successful. So I watched his video, then I bought his book, and I started to think that I could achieve the same goals, because I could see someone else doing it.

ADAM: A really good leader is someone who works hard to build relationships, befriending people just so they can help them. I was lucky enough to hand over the title of Australian of the Year to Rosie Batty in 2015, and she is a fantastic leader. She makes me very proud. I'm very inspired by her strength as a single mother and the trauma that she's been through.

I am more inspired by people who overcome adversity than by those who just do the job that is expected of them. Other leaders I've enjoyed looking up to are my coaches, because they have really challenged me and supported me to get better. Paul Roos would always congratulate me when I did something well.

MICHAEL: Adam is probably as good as they get in terms of leaders today. But I've been fortunate enough to be around great leaders at the Swans. Guys like

Paul Kelly, a champion player who didn't necessarily say that much, but led by example in the way he trained. He set an example of 'This is how you do it!' And when he spoke, everyone listened.

ADAM: I have reached the goals I've set in the past, and I'm now setting new goals that I will look at every six months. It's good to have goals. If your goal is to fly a rocket-ship, then you need to understand the process that you have to go through to become a pilot. You need to get good grades in school, go to university, do the training, and do all the simulations. It takes planning. When you are really clear, and when you write down your goals and tell them to someone else, it makes them more real. It is more likely that you will stay on track to reach them. If you tell your teachers, your parents or someone else you respect what your goals are, then they can help you on that journey.

MICHAEL: I have goals. I want to be a successful business owner. I want to run a cleaning business. I want to learn about the process of being a businessman. I know that becoming a proud business owner is like anything else: you've got to put the work in and the outcomes will follow.

My goals have changed since I was a footballer, and now I have kids. But when you don't hit your goals it's about readjusting. It's about persevering and persisting with the roadblocks and the hurdles you encounter, so you can achieve your goals.

For example, everything about becoming a footballer was tough for me: I was really poor at running, I was really skinny and I didn't eat the right food. So to become an AFL player meant the person I was at seventeen and the person I became at twenty were two completely different people, because of the journey I went on. There were times when I just wanted to give up and go back to

Adelaide, and be with my friends as they were celebrating eighteenth birthday parties and their twenty-first parties. I was still training on my own twenty-first.

But I have no regrets. It was all worth it in the end. Sometimes I didn't hit my goals, but at least I could look at myself in the mirror and say, 'Well, it didn't work out this time, but at least I gave myself every chance to be successful'. I'm a big believer in preparation, preparation and preparation. If you get that right, then ultimately you'll become successful.

ADAM: One of the things I always wanted to do was to jump out of an airplane – and I did it! It was incredible! I was quite calm until I put my feet and legs over the side, and then I just fell out and freefell for about a minute and a half. It was so enjoyable and so much fun. I would definitely do it again.

One day I'd like to go to Africa to see the beautiful animals in the wild. It's truly beautiful countryside. I'd like to have a family, too, and to be a good father.

MICHAEL: One thing I really want to do is attend the NBA final series. I'd also like to go to every major sporting event in the world!

ADAM: I believe in having a dream and setting goals to achieve it. If you really want to be the best at anything, then you have to have the knowledge to do that. So you need role models, you need to be a good listener, to learn from your elders (people who have done it before). You have to have a great work ethic, and most importantly you need to have fun and love what you are doing.

MICHAEL: To be a professional footballer, you have to work hard, train hard and sacrifice things like going out. You need to study hard and go to school — these are the biggest things you need to do. Finally, I'd say you need to dedicate your energies towards striving to be the best.

Anita Heiss

Anita Heiss has written a LOT of books
for kids and adults. She writes about
history, sport, naughty dogs, women
who like shopping and politics, and
sometimes she writes travel stories.
Anita thinks reading is very important,
which is why she is an ambassador for
the Indigenous Literacy Foundation.
She's won four Deadly Awards for her
writing and just being deadly. In 2012

Anita was a finalist in the Human Rights Award, and in 2013 she was a finalist in the Australian of the Year Awards. Anita lives in Brisbane, and she loves running and chocolate.

Adam Goodes

Adam Goodes played his first game for the Sydney Swans in 1999, when he was nineteen, and he won the AFL Rising Star Award that year. He went on to play 372 games for the Swans, taking the mantle of games record holder from his mate Micky O! He won two Brownlow Medals, was named his club's best-and-fairest player three times, was four times All-Australian, captained the Australian

International Rules team, and was a member of the AFL's Indigenous Team of the Century. In 2009 Adam co-founded the GO Foundation alongside Michael.

In recognition of his community work and his commitment to campaign against racism, Adam was named Australian of the Year in 2014.

Michael O'Loughlin

Michael O'Loughlin played his first game for the Sydney Swans in 1995 at the age of eighteen. In total he played 303 senior games for the club, including three AFL Grand Finals. He was named the club's best-and-fairest player in 1998, was twice All-Australian, twice represented Australia in International Rules, and was a member of the AFL's Indigenous Team of the Century. Since hanging up his boots he has continued to be involved with football, most recently as the head coach of the QBE Swans Academy. In 2009 he co-founded the GO Foundation, alongside Adam.

KICKING GOALS FOR LIFE

www.go-foundation.org

Our Vision

The GO Foundation exists to provide Indigenous children with scholarships to quality schools, and to meet expenses for students attending these schools. We believe that education is the single most important factor in Indigenous Australians achieving a brighter future. Education is the cornerstone of a healthy, happy and productive life, and its benefits are immeasurable.

According to the 2006 census, only 19% of Indigenous Australians had completed schooling to Year 12 or equivalent, compared with 45% of non-Indigenous Australians.

In partnership with the Australian Indigenous Education Foundation, the GO Foundation identifies students who will benefit from assistance to obtain a quality education.

These scholarships are for local kids who would otherwise not be able to access quality schooling, and we are committed to assisting these kids with their educational needs for the duration of their school education.

The Story So Far

When we started GO, we were a couple of young men trying to save the world. We might have made some mistakes, but we had the best of intentions.

Michael O'Loughlin, April 2014

The GO Foundation burst into life in 2009 in the NSW town of Dareton. With a population of approximately 600, around a third of whom are of Indigenous or Torres Strait Islander heritage, Dareton became the focus of GO's initial foray into community work.

During the following three years, the Foundation participated in various community programmes, ranging from presentations on healthy lifestyle to vocational training for Indigenous students.

Our ongoing involvement with the Dareton community saw numerous achievements, including the donation of sports uniforms and equipment to local schools, as well as $20,000 worth of playground equipment and fencing for the local community centre.

To become involved in a regional Indigenous community taught us a great deal about what a difference the GO Foundation can make in the lives of our people, and how we can best achieve positive change.

In 2012, the Foundation refined its focus to an area in which lasting results could be achieved – education. Both Michael and Adam firmly believe that education of Indigenous girls and boys is at the heart of GO's mission.

The GO Foundation established its current Board in 2013, and worked towards establishing the platform for providing scholarships for Indigenous students for years 9 to 12.

To that end, GO formed a partnership with the Australian Indigenous Education Foundation (AIEF), Australia's leading Indigenous education administrator. AIEF also incorporates a mentoring and career pathway function, which introduces students to job and career opportunities following their education.

Additionally, the GO Foundation enhanced its association with the Sydney Swans – a natural fit given the relationship of the club with Adam and Michael. The Sydney Swans provide administrative support for the GO Foundation, with the two brands having a greater community and partnership reach as a result of this association.